Contents

KU-362-416

Sudden landing!

A speeding plane comes in to land on a ship. Will it stop in time? Or will it splash into the ocean? Suddenly, a hook on the plane catches wires on the ship. The plane stops in time!

hook

DID YOU KNOW?

The aeroplane is moving at 240 km (150 miles) per hour when it starts to land. But it stops in just two seconds!

Floating cities

Aircaft carriers are big **warships** that planes can land on. Planes fly to and from the aircraft carrier to protect a country and fight enemies. Thousands of people live and work on these ships. They are like small cities.

An aircraft carrier has enough room for a basketball court!

Who lands a plane on a ship?

Navy **pilots** have exciting jobs. But landing on aircraft carriers can be scary. Pilots train, or practise, landing on aircraft carriers. They also practise taking off!

DID YOU KNOW?

Pilots wait to hear from the aircraft carrier that it is safe to land.

Into enemy territory!

Pilots on aircraft carriers help their country fight wars. They fly planes over enemy land. They find out what the enemy is doing. They can drop **bombs** from the air to destroy enemies. Pilots also help to protect people.

Pilots in planes help
protect soldiers on
the ground.

The flight deck

The top level of an aircraft carrier is called the **flight deck**. Workers on the flight deck use a machine called a **catapult**. It helps blast aeroplanes into the sky.

DID YOU KNOW?

An aircraft carrier can hold 80 planes!

catapult

Some say the flight deck is one of the most dangerous places in the world. Planes with weapons are always zooming by. The **catapult** officer guides the pilots using body signals.

Aircraft carrier body signals

• Raised fists mean "brakes on."

• Leaning forward and pointing means "launch."

Preparing planes

The **hangar deck** is below the **flight deck**. It is like a big garage for planes. Many people work on the hangar deck. Mechanics fix planes. Workers pump fuel into planes. Some workers bring planes up to the flight deck on lifts.

lift

DID YOU KNOW?

U.S. Navy workers who pump fuel into planes wear purple shirts. They are called "grapes."

Powerful weapons

Aircraft carriers are **warships**. They need **weapons** to protect the ship. The people who work with weapons have very dangerous jobs. Workers carefully load weapons onto planes.

Some weapons can
explode if they aren't
handled carefully!

The air boss

A tall building called an island is at one end of the aircraft carrier. A person called the **air boss** directs takeoffs and landings here. As many as two planes per minute can take off. The air boss must always pay attention.

island

Who's in control?

About 5,000 men and women live on an aircraft carrier. They sail for months before returning to land. Someone must make sure everyone does their job.

The **captain** is the leader of the ship. Everyone follows the captain's orders.

Caring for sick people

Doctors live and work on an aircraft carrier. They take care of everyone's health. There is even a hospital on the ship. If someone is very ill or hurt in battle, doctors can perform operations.

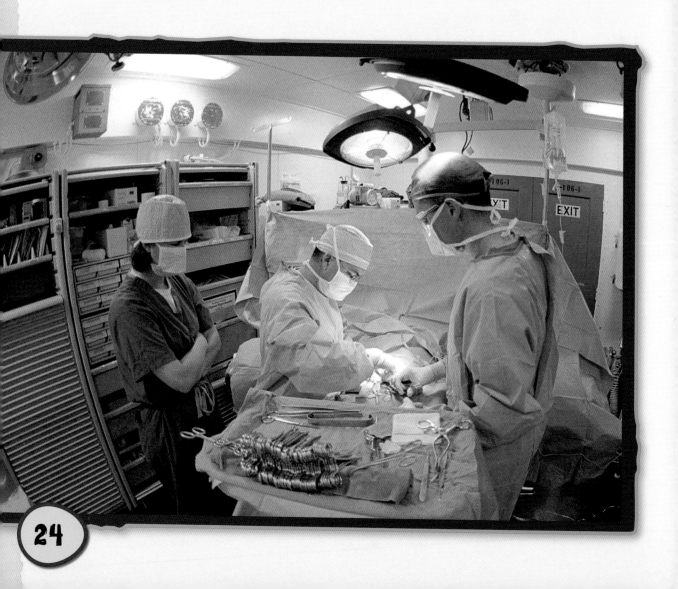

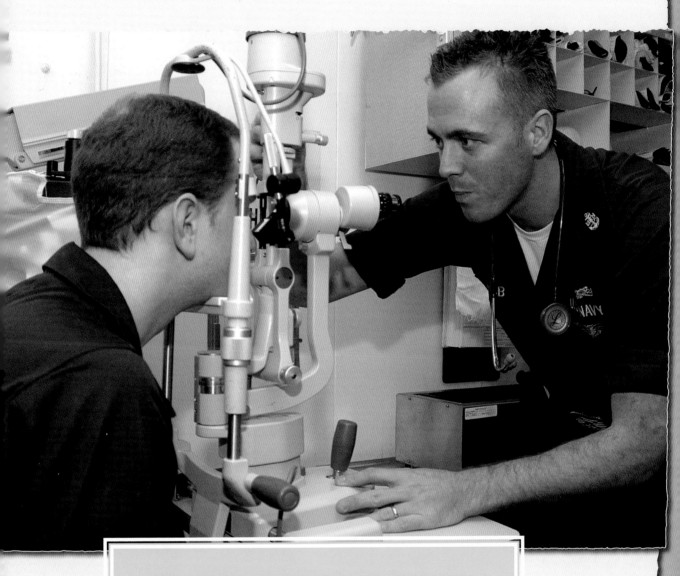

Aeroplane pilots must have perfect vision. This doctor is testing his patient's eyesight.

To the rescue!

Everyone on a ship is careful. But accidents can still happen. Aircraft carriers must be ready for **emergencies**. They even have firefighters on the ship! If a fire starts, these firefighters can quickly put it out.

Helicopters rescue
people who fall into
the sea.

Could you work on an aircraft carrier?

Would you like living on a floating city? Do you think and act quickly in **emergencies**? To become a **pilot**, you have to work and study hard for many years. It's worth it if you want the thrill of flying speeding planes onto an aircraft carrier.

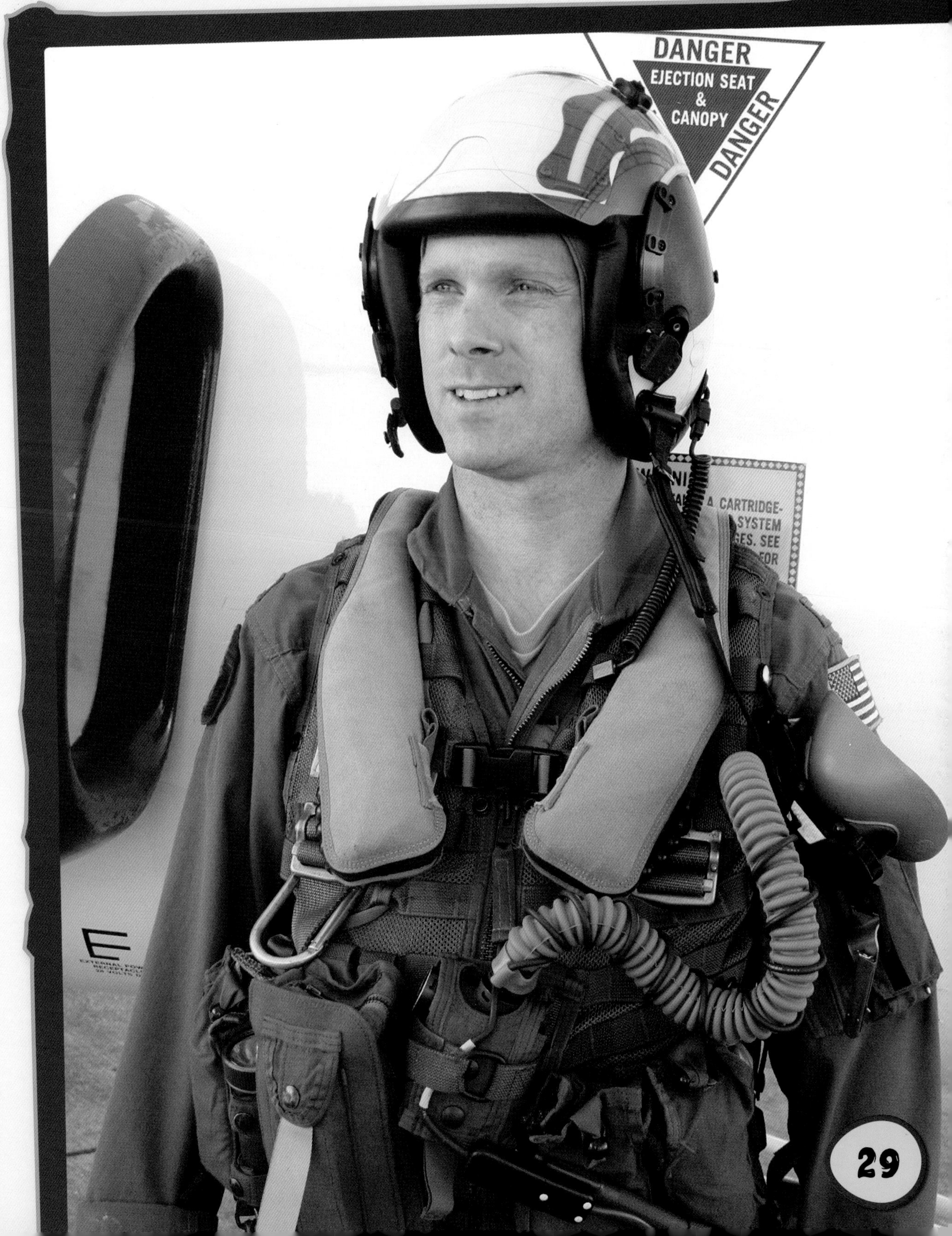
DANGER
EJECTION SEAT
&
CANOPY
DANGER

Glossary

air boss the person on an aircraft carrier who directs aeroplane takeoffs and landings

bomb a weapon that explodes

captain the person in charge on an aircraft carrier

catapult a machine that helps to get an aeroplane into the sky from an aircraft carrier

emergencies situations that are sudden and serious

flight deck the top level of an aircraft carrier where planes take off and land

hangar deck a deck, or level, of an aircraft carrier where aeroplanes are stored

pilot a person who flies an aeroplane

warship large ship made especially for fighting

weapon something used to harm others or protect yourself

Find out more

Books to read

Aircraft Carriers, Lynn M. Stone (Rourke, 2007)

Fighter Pilot, Jameson Anderson (Raintree, 2006)

Fighter Pilot, Stephen Rickard (Ransom Publishing, 2010)

Websites to visit

The Royal Navy
http://www.royalnavy.mod.uk/operations-and-support/surface-fleet/aircraft-carriers/
Learn about aircraft carriers used by the Royal Navy. and watch a video of life onboard an aircraft carrier.

Northrop Grumman's USS *George H.W. Bush* page
http://www.nn.northropgrumman.com/bush/kids.html
This website has fun facts about US Navy aircraft carriers.

Index